Folktales from Asia

Folktales from Asia

Selected by
Michael Collins

Illustrated by
Alana Bhattacharya

This edition published in the United States of America in 2000 by
MONDO Publishing
By arrangement with MULTIMEDIA
INTERNATIONAL (UK) LTD

For information contact:
MONDO Publishing
980 Avenue of the Americas
New York, New York 10018

Printed in Singapore
First Mondo printing, January 2000
02 03 04 05 9 8 7 6 5 4 3 2

ISBN 1-57255-788-5
Original development by Snowball Educational
Designed by Mina Greenstein
Production by The Kids at Our House

Contents

Introduction

The folktales in this book come from Asia, that part of the world whose two largest countries are China and India. Asia is the home of some very old civilizations, rich in literature, art, and music. However, until recent times, most of the people living there led simple lives as small farmers. The seven folktales in this book are about such people.

Folktales were developed when few people could read or write and stories were told, not written. These stories provided simple explanations for things which could not be explained scientifically. For example, *Why Dogs and Cats Are Enemies* attempts to fathom a common truth, which is that dogs do not like cats. Asian folktales were passed far and wide across the countryside and down through time from generation to generation by word of mouth. Children would continually hear these stories from their parents and grandparents, partly for their entertainment but also for their education.

Because people in Asia believed in magic and miracles, some of their folktales are about supernatural beings, demons, and monsters. Several moral themes run through these stories. Creatures who are good, hardworking, thoughtful, and brave triumph in the end, as you will see in *A Crippled Boy* and *How Ba Kho Killed the Monster with Four Mouths*. The virtues of honesty, wisdom, and kindness to people and animals are rewarded, while greed, stupidity, laziness, and cruelty are punished.

I hope you will enjoy reading or hearing these folktales. For those who pause to think, a message of wisdom can be found in every one.

My-Van Tran
Lecturer in South-East Asian History and Civilizations, Darwin Institute of Technology

The Parrot

(a story from China)

Once upon a time there was a man named Liu Ge who had a parrot. Every morning the parrot would fly to Liu Ge's bed and call to him, "Good morning, Brother! Good morning, Brother!" Liu Ge loved the parrot very much and wherever he went, he always took the parrot with him.

One year the district magistrate wanted to build a new house. Liu Ge went to work for the district magistrate and every day he took the parrot with him.

While Liu Ge was working, the parrot perched on one side and watched. And when Liu Ge was high up carving patterns in the woodwork, the parrot would call out to him, "Be careful, Brother! Be careful, Brother!" All the carpenters loved the parrot and they often taught it to talk and to sing.

One day the district magistrate came to see how the work was going. Just as he stepped inside the door, he heard a voice saying, "Nice work! Nice work!" He looked up. The voice came from the parrot who was perched on a crossbeam.

"Whose parrot is this?" demanded the district magistrate.

"It's mine," replied Liu Ge.

"Good," smiled the district magistrate. He took a look around at the work and then he left.

The following day, the district magistrate's steward came

to see Liu Ge. "My master likes that parrot very much," said the steward. "He orders you to hand it over to him and in return he will give you some pieces of silver."

"Oh, no!" replied Liu Ge. "The parrot is not for sale."

The steward begged Liu Ge until he was blue in the face, but still Liu Ge would not agree to hand over the parrot. There was nothing more the steward could do and so he returned to report to his master.

A few days later, Liu Ge was carving a panel at the house. Suddenly, the district magistrate and several of his officials charged into the house. "Come on! Grab the parrot!" he cried. The officials threw themselves at the parrot, trying to catch it.

"You can't have it," cried Liu Ge. As he battled with the officials, he shouted to the bird, "Quick, parrot, fly away!"

The parrot flew back and forth, followed by the officials. At last, with a loud cry, it flew away.

The district magistrate was very angry. Since he was unable to catch the parrot, he threw Liu Ge into jail.

The parrot was very lonely without Liu Ge. Every day it asked about him and every day it went to look for him. One day it made its way into Liu Ge's cell through a hole in the wall. Out it hopped onto Liu Ge, who was overjoyed to see it again.

"Oh, parrot!" cried Liu Ge. "Where have you been? The district magistrate beats me every day. He has tortured me and broken my hand. He tries to force me to hand you over to him but I still refuse." The parrot nodded. From that day on, the parrot came to see Liu Ge every day. But the officials heard what was happening and reported it to the district magistrate.

One night the officials, led by the district magistrate, rushed into Liu Ge's cell to catch the parrot. The parrot flew up to a beam and called down, "The great magistrate bullies the people, but he can't touch me!" And with that, the parrot flew away. The district magistrate was so angry that his beard stood on end.

The following night, the parrot came again to Liu Ge's cell. As they were talking happily together, a group of officials suddenly surrounded them on all sides. This time the parrot could not escape.

"Ha! Ha!" the district magistrate laughed loudly. "Now that I have caught you, I am going to eat you!"

"Go ahead," the parrot replied. "One day I shall feed your bones to the wild dogs."

"Grr!" roared the district magistrate. "Take this bird away at once and fry it in oil!"

As soon as the cook got the parrot, he plucked out all of its feathers. But as he turned around to pour the oil into the pan, the parrot seized its chance to escape. It flapped its wings but it could not fly. With a tremendous effort, it hopped out of the kitchen through a hole and down into the drainpipes.

The parrot's feathers took a long, long time to grow back again. When they did grow back, the parrot flew all over town searching for Liu Ge. But Liu Ge was nowhere to be found. He had escaped from prison and now lived as a farmer in the mountains.

One day the parrot was flying up and down above the main street in town. Suddenly, it heard the sound of gongs. The district magistrate was going to the temple. The parrot had an idea.

While the district magistrate was at the temple, he heard a voice coming from one of the idols saying, "Now everyone in town talks about your evil deeds!" When he heard the voice, the district magistrate was very frightened.

"Be quick and confess all your wicked deeds," continued the idol. "That way I may still forgive you. But if you do not confess, beware for your life!" The district magistrate fell to the ground and kowtowed again and again to the idol saying, "No! No! I will tell all!"

As he kowtowed, the district magistrate told of all his wicked deeds. "Ha!" the idol said. "You have been so evil that I cannot forgive you. . . ." The district magistrate kowtowed even harder and begged, "Have mercy on me! Have mercy on me!"

The idol paused for a while and then continued, "Since you have confessed all of your mistakes, I will spare your life and I will give you only the lightest of punishments." When the district magistrate heard this, he breathed a sigh of relief.

"Now, listen!" said the idol. "First, you must pluck out all the hair in your beard right here and now. Without your fine beard, you will not be able to give yourself so many airs." The district magistrate obeyed at once and plucked out every single hair of his beard.

"And second," continued the idol, "kowtow to me three hundred and sixty times so you know how it feels." The district magistrate dared not delay. He began to kowtow at once. He kowtowed so long and so hard that eventually a big lump swelled up on his head.

All of a sudden a voice said, "Do you see who I am? Last year you plucked out my feathers and this year you've plucked out your beard. You broke Liu Ge's hand last year and this year, you've broken your own pighead."

The district magistrate looked up and stamped his foot in anger. But the parrot was already out of reach, flying away high up in the sky.

Why Dogs and Cats Are Enemies

(a story from Java)

A long time ago, all animals were friends and they lived peacefully together. They helped each other as much as they could and never fought among themselves or hurt one another.

One day, however, a special meeting was called so that all the animals could talk about how things might be in the future. The lion was the chairman. He was about to declare the meeting open when he noticed that the camel was missing. Not wishing to start without the camel, he asked the assembled animals if they knew where he was. Since no one knew, the lion became alarmed, fearing that some trouble was keeping the camel from attending. He asked if any of the animals would go and look for the camel.

Immediately, the dog jumped up and volunteered. He was proud of his ability, and felt certain he could find the camel quickly. The only trouble was he had never seen the camel before, so he did not know what the camel looked like.

"Mr. Chairman," the dog said. "I'll find the camel for you, if you'll just tell me what he looks like."

"The camel is easy to find," replied the lion, "because he has a large hump on his back."

This information seemed enough for the dog and he raced

off to find the camel. Now it happened that, by chance, the cat was also absent from the meeting, but the lion hadn't noticed. The cat was running full tilt towards the meeting while the dog was speeding away from the meeting. Their paths crossed near some bushes and they collided heavily.

The cat recovered immediately but was so startled that she arched her back in fear as cats will do. Seeing the arched back, the dog immediately concluded that it was a natural hump and that he had met the camel.

"Come on, friend," he gasped. "You're late for the meeting. Come along with me now."

Not wanting to argue, the cat joined the dog, and the two of them raced side by side towards the meeting place. When they burst upon the assembled animals, they created quite a stir because everyone was expecting the camel and here instead was the cat. At first a few giggled, but in a few moments, all the animals were roaring with laughter at the dog's mistake.

Of course the dog was puzzled at the animals' reaction, and he wanted to know why they were laughing at him.

"Well," answered the lion, "they were expecting to see the camel, and you have brought the cat. Have a look. This animal has no hump."

The dog quickly glanced at the cat. It was quite true: there was no hump. Immediately the dog grew furious, suspecting that the cat had deliberately tricked him. Without a moment's thought, the dog bared his teeth and sprang at the cat. But the cat was alert and dodged the attack. When the dog prepared to attack a second time, the cat leaped for safety up the nearest tree.

Not being able to climb trees, the dog could not follow the cat. But he sat below the tree, trembling with anger and shame, and made a solemn promise:

"Cat! From this day on, we will be enemies. My descendants will attack your descendants forever and ever, and kill them when they can."

And so it is that dogs and cats are still enemies.

LAZY TOK

(a story from Borneo)

PART I

Tok was born lazy. When she was a baby, everyone said what a good baby she was because she never cried. But, really, she was too lazy to cry. It was too much trouble. The older she grew, the lazier she became until she was too tired to go and look for food for herself. One day she was sitting by the side of the river, too lazy to wonder where her next meal was coming from, when a nipa tree on the other side of the river spoke to her. A nipa tree is a kind of palm tree.

"Good evening, Tok," it said. "Would you like to know how to get your meals without having to work for them?"

Tok was too lazy to answer, but she nodded her head.

"Well, come over here and I'll tell you," said the nipa tree.

"Oh, I'm much too weary to come over there. Couldn't you come here?" yawned Tok.

"Very well," said the nipa tree. And it bent over the river. "Just tear off one of my branches," it said.

"Oh, what a bother," said Tok. "Couldn't you shake one down yourself?"

So the nipa tree shook itself and down dropped one of its branches at Tok's feet.

"Good evening, Tok," said the nipa branch. "Would you

like to be able to get your meals without having to work for them?"

Tok was too lazy to answer, but she nodded her head.

"Well," said the nipa branch, "all you have to do is make a basket out of me."

"What a bother," said Tok. "Couldn't you make yourself into a basket without my help?"

"Oh, very well," said the nipa branch. And it made itself into a nice, neat, wide, fat basket.

"Good evening, Tok," said the basket. "Would you like to be able to get your meals without having to work for them?"

Tok was too lazy to answer, but she nodded her head.

"Then pick me up," said the basket, "and carry me to the edge of the road and leave me there."

"Couldn't you pick yourself up and go without bothering me?" asked Tok.

"Oh, very well," said the basket. And it picked itself up and went off to lie down by the side of the road.

PART II

The basket hadn't been waiting there long before an overweight man came along.

"What luck!" said the man. "Here's a fine basket that somebody has dropped. It's perfect for me to carry my food home from the market."

So he picked up the basket and went off to the market with it. He soon piled it high with rice, potatoes, dried shrimp, and other things too numerous to mention. When it was filled up, he started to walk home.

After a while, he felt hot and tired. He put the basket down under a tree and dozed. As soon as the basket saw that the man was fast asleep, it jumped up and ran to Lazy Tok.

"Here I am," said the basket. "Here I am, filled to the brim. All you have to do is to empty me out and you will have enough food to last you for a week."

"Dear, oh, dear!" said Lazy Tok. "What a bother! Couldn't you empty yourself out?"

"Oh, very well," said the basket cheerfully, and it emptied itself into Tok's lap.

The next week, when Tok had eaten all the food, the basket went off again and lay down on the grass by the side of the road. This time an older man came along. When he saw the basket, he thought it would be fine to carry his food home from the market. So he picked it up and took it with him. When it was full of pineapples and all sorts of nice things too numerous to mention, he started for home with it. But he hadn't gone far before he felt tired and hot, and sat down on the side of the road to have a nap. As soon as he had fallen asleep, the basket jumped up and ran home to Lazy Tok.

Every week the basket carried itself to the market and came back full of fruit and rice and all sorts of other nice things too numerous to mention. And Lazy Tok sat on the river bank and ate and ate and ate and got fatter and fatter and lazier and lazier until she became so fat and so lazy that she simply couldn't feed herself.

"Here we are, waiting to be eaten," said the fruit and the shrimp and the other nice things one day.

"Oh, bother," said Lazy Tok. "Couldn't you feed me yourself, without giving me so much trouble?"

"We'll try," said the fruit and the shrimp and the other nice things. After that, they would drop into her mouth without giving her any trouble.

PART III

Lazy Tok grew fatter and FATTER and FATTER and lazier and LAZIER and LAZIER. One day the basket went off to lie down by the side of the road. Just then the overweight man, who had picked it up the first time, came along.

"Twee!" he said angrily. "There you are, you thief!" And he picked up the basket and took it to the market to show all his friends what had been robbing them. His friends came to look at the basket and cried, "This is the rascal that has been robbing us!"

They took the basket and filled it with soldier ants, lizards, hot-footed scorpions, bees, wasps, leeches, and all sorts of other creeping, prickling, biting, stinging, tickling, and itchy things far too unpleasant to mention. Then, they let the basket go.

The basket ran, with its load of bugs and beetles and centipedes and gnats, straight home to Lazy Tok.

"What have you got for me today?" asked Lazy Tok.

"You'd better get up and look," said the basket.

"Oh, dear me, no!" said Tok. "I'm so tired, and I can't lift a finger. Just empty yourself into my lap."

So the basket emptied the ants and beetles, and other things too horrible to mention, into Lazy Tok's lap.

Lazy Tok got up and ran and ran and ran, as she had never run in her life before. But the ants, beetles, and scorpions ran after her, and the leeches and lizards crawled after her, and the wasps and bees flew after her. They stung her and bit her and pricked her. The harder she ran, the harder they bit her. As far as I know she may still be running, and she is thinner than ever.

How the Man in the Moon Found a Friend

(a story from Japan)

A very long, long time ago, a great green forest covered the earth. Around the forest was the deep blue sea. And above the forest and the sea was the great blue sky.

There were all kinds of fish in the sea—great-sized fish, middle-sized fish, small-sized fish, and many tiny fish. And all of the fish were friends with each other. And that was as it should be.

There were all kinds of animals in the great green forest—great-sized animals, middle-sized animals, and many tiny animals. And all of the animals were friends with each other. And that was as it should be.

There were all the stars and all the planets and the great sun and the great moon in the great blue sky. Now, no one lived on the stars. And as far as anyone knew, no one lived on the planets. And, of course, no one lived on the sun (because it was too hot). But someone lived on the moon. And he was the Old-Man-in-the-Moon. And he had no one else with him at all. He was a very lonely Old-Man-in-the-Moon. And that was not as it should be.

He looked down at the fish in the sea and they all had friends! He wished with all of his heart that he had a friend, too.

One day he saw a monkey, a rabbit, and a fox playing in the forest. They were playing games with one another. They were playing hide-and-seek. They were chasing each other. They were telling each other jokes. They were laughing a lot and having a wonderful time. The Old-Man-in-the-Moon could see that they were very good friends.

"Perhaps the monkey or the fox or the rabbit would be my special friend," said the Old-Man-in-the-Moon. "I must find out which one of them is the finest."

The Old-Man-in-the-Moon disguised himself as a poor wanderer and went down into the forest.

The monkey and the rabbit and the fox were busy chasing each other's tails. Round and round they went until the monkey caught the fox's red bushy tail and the rabbit caught the monkey's curly gray tail and the fox caught the rabbit's little white bobtail.

Then they looked at each other and fell on the ground laughing. They really did look very funny! Just then, they saw the poor old wanderer (who was really the Old-Man-in-the-Moon). They could see that he was very tired. He walked very slowly towards them.

"I'm sorry to interrupt your game," he said to them. "But

could you let me have some food? I have come a long way and I am so hungry."

The monkey and the rabbit and the fox felt quite sorry for the poor wanderer. "Of course, we will give you some food," they said. "You rest here and we will find some for you."

Off they went. The monkey climbed up into the highest branches of the forest trees. "The fruit is sweeter up here," he said. He picked fat, yellow bananas and red, juicy berries. He wrapped them carefully in young leaves to keep them fresh. Then he balanced a bright orange melon on top of his head and scampered carefully back to the old wanderer.

"Thank you, dear monkey. This looks delicious," said the old wanderer. He peeled off the bright yellow skin from a fat banana and started to eat it.

Meanwhile the fox bounded through the forest until he came to a deep, clear pool. "I know there are many fat fish here," he said. He stood on the very edge of a rock and put his snout over the edge. He waited patiently for the fat fish to swim by. Sure enough, they came right by his nose and soon he caught a big fish. "This will do very nicely for the poor wanderer," said the fox, and he happily carried the fish back through the forest.

The poor wanderer was very satisfied when he saw the fat fish the fox had brought him. "Thank you, dear fox," he said. "This will make a fine meal."

Just then, the rabbit hopped out of the bushes. His long, pointed ears drooped over his face and he looked quite sad. "I have looked every single place there is to look," he cried. "And I have not found any food for you! Oh, what can I do?"

The rabbit thought very hard. Suddenly, his long ears sprang right up. "I have an idea!" He started hopping around, picking up sticks. He built a big fire and when the fire was very bright, he said to the poor wanderer, "Since I could not find anything for you, I will hop on this fire and you can have rabbit stew for your supper."

"No, no, no, little rabbit!" said the poor wanderer and he scooped the rabbit up in his arms. "You are a very, very kind little rabbit, but you should never do anything to harm yourself."

And in a flash, the poor wanderer threw off his disguise.

"You are the Old-Man-in-the-Moon!" cried the monkey and the rabbit and the fox together. "Why have you come to the forest?"

The old man carefully sat down. "I have come because I am a very lonely Old-Man-in-the-Moon," he said, and he stroked the rabbit's long, soft ears. "I am looking for a very special friend. I am looking for a very kind friend." He spoke very softly to the rabbit. "Dear rabbit, you are the kindest friend I have found. Will you come to the moon and be my friend?"

The rabbit was indeed kind, and right away he said, "I would very much like to be your friend, Old-Man-in-the-Moon. And I will be happy to go to the moon with you. But all the same, I will be very sad if I do not see the monkey and the fox again, so you must promise me that I may come back to Earth and visit them as often as possible."

The Old-Man-in-the-Moon agreed, and the rabbit gave the monkey and the fox a big hug each, and they all chased each other one special last time in order to say good-bye. Then the Old-Man-in-the-Moon carried the rabbit in his arms all the way up to the sky and put him on the moon.

And there they are, the old man and the rabbit, to this very day. If you look carefully one bright, starry night, you might see them. But if, one night when you're looking very hard, the rabbit isn't there, he is almost certain to be visiting his friends, the monkey and the fox.

And that, my friends, is how it should be.

A Crippled Boy

(a story from Vietnam)

Long, long ago there was a boy named Theo. He was crippled in both legs and could hardly walk. Since he could not work, he had no choice but to live on rice and vegetables which kind people gave him.

Often he sat watching other children play and run about. Unable to join them, he felt very miserable. To amuse himself, Theo practiced throwing pebbles at targets. Hour after hour, he would spend practicing his aim. Having nothing else to do, he soon learned to hit all his targets. Other children took pity on him and gave him more pebbles to throw. Theo could also make all sorts of shapes with stones on the ground.

One hot day, Theo sat under a big banyan tree whose thick leaves gave him a lovely, cool shade. He aimed stones at the thick foliage and managed to cut it into the outlines of animal forms. He was very pleased at what he could do and soon forgot his loneliness. Under the tree, he watched the shadows of the leaves on the ground.

One day, Theo was under his favorite banyan tree. To his surprise, he heard a drumbeat. Soon he saw many men in official clothes. It happened that the king was out for a country walk with some of his officials and was passing by Theo's tree.

The king's attention was caught by the unusual shadow of the tree. He stopped and was very surprised to see little, crippled Theo sitting there all alone. Theo was very frightened and tried to get away, but he could not crawl very far. The king asked Theo what he had been doing. Theo told the king his story. Then the king asked Theo to demonstrate his skill at pebble throwing. Theo was happy to do so. The king was impressed and asked Theo to return with him to the palace where, the king said, "I have a little job for you to do."

The following day, the king had a meeting with his aides and ordered Theo to sit quietly behind a curtain. The king had ordered a few holes to be made in the curtain so that Theo could see what was going on. The king explained, "Most of my aides talk too much. They never bother to listen to me or let me finish my sentence. So if anybody opens his mouth to speak while I am talking, just throw a pebble into his mouth. This will teach him to keep quiet."

Sure enough, just as the meeting was about to start, one aide opened his mouth, ready to speak. Oops! Something flew into his mouth and he quickly closed it. Another aide opened his mouth to speak but strangely enough he, too, shut his mouth without saying a word. A miracle had happened. Throughout the entire meeting, all of the aides were silent. For once, the king could speak as much as he wanted without being interrupted. The king was so pleased with Theo's help that he treasured his presence and service in the palace forever after.

Theo remained happily at the palace, no longer needing to beg for food and no longer sitting alone under the banyan tree.

How Ba Kho Killed the Monster with Four Mouths

(a story from Vietnam)

Once a terrible monster lived in a village. Everyone was afraid of the monster because it ate people. It had four mouths to eat up its victims, and five noses to smell where they might be hiding.

This terrible monster went out every night, looking for people to eat. Nobody could kill it because the monster ate everyone who came near it.

Finally, the villagers held a meeting. They decided that each family in turn should offer a person to be eaten by the monster. In this way, they hoped the monster would kill only one person a day, instead of several in a single night. Everyone agreed to this plan except a young man named Ba Kho, which means "the poor one."

Although Ba Kho was indeed poor, he was also brave and cunning. "We must kill the monster," he said. "We must not give in." But everyone was afraid of the monster.

"The monster has killed four of our best and strongest swordsmen," said the people. "Who would dare to fight him now?"

"I will fight him," said Ba Kho, "but I need help. Who will help me?"

Nobody answered. They knew Ba Kho was not a swordsman, and they did not think anyone could kill the monster. Instead they began to offer the monster one victim every day. Now, the monster stopped going out at night looking for people to eat. It stayed at home and waited for its victims to be brought to it. It grew fat and lazy.

One day the villagers told Ba Kho's family that in one week, it would be their turn to offer a victim to the monster. "I will go," said Ba Kho, "and I will kill the monster!"

Ba Kho took a knife with a long, wide blade and went to the crossroads. There he sharpened his knife. When people passed by, they said, "Ba Kho, what are you doing?" And Ba Kho replied, "I am sharpening my knife to kill the monster. Will you come and help me?" But when the people heard the word "monster," they hurried away, and Ba Kho was left alone.

At last a funny man with a long, round body hopped up to Ba Kho. He was very big at the top and very small at the feet and was dressed in bright, red clothes. On his head, he wore a small, green hat.

"Good morning, Ba Kho," he said. "I am King Chili, the king of all the chili plants. May I ask why you are sharpening that knife?"

"I am going to kill the monster," said Ba Kho. "Why don't you help me? The monster has trampled upon so many of your subjects that soon there will be none left."

"But how can a weak person like me kill the monster?" asked King Chili.

"We are weak," said Ba Kho, "but if there are many of us, we will be strong. Go and bring back some of your friends."

King Chili hopped away, and just then King Bee came buzzing by. Ba Kho told him he was going to kill the monster. "Why don't you help?" said Ba Kho. "The monster has stolen your honey and killed your subjects."

"I will, I will," cried King Bee.

"Then go and ask some of your friends," said Ba Kho, "because if there are many of us, our task will be easier."

The next day King Chili and King Bee came back, each with a friend. King Chili brought King Moss, who was very thin and wore ragged green clothes. King Bee came with King Snake, who looked just like a snake.

While they were talking about how they might best kill the monster, two other creatures joined them. One had a very big head, and his name was King Pumpkin. He did not walk, but only rolled along. The other wore heavy armor and walked very slowly. He was King Tortoise. They were also very angry with the monster and they agreed to join the fight.

While they were still talking, King Fox and King Monkey strolled by. "Just the ones we need," cried Ba Kho. "With the help of such clever creatures as King Fox and King Monkey, we will surely defeat the monster."

King Fox was very pleased at being called clever and agreed to join at once. But King Monkey refused because the monster had not bothered any monkeys so far.

Then Ba Kho and his companions thought out a plan to destroy the monster. They spoke in whispers for they did not want anyone to hear them. At last, the plan was complete and Ba Kho and his companions separated. They agreed to meet later that night.

That night, the monster ate his victim as usual and drank a lot of wine. Then he went to bed. Soon his snores filled the house.

When the monster was fast asleep, Ba Kho and his friends gathered as silently as shadows in front of the house. Some climbed on the roof, others slid into the kitchen, and some hid in the garden.

When the rooster crowed, Ba Kho was ready. He stood at the foot of the stairs to the monster's front door. His knife gleamed in his hand.

Right on time, King Fox broke into the hen house and began chasing the hens. The hens made a terrible noise and woke up the monster. "Who dares to steal my hens?" he roared. "I'll eat you alive."

With that, the monster threw off his blanket and jumped out of bed. But King Snake was waiting for him under the bed. He bit the monster's big toe and coiled himself around his leg.

"Ow!" shrieked the monster. But it was dark in his room and he could not see King Snake. So he ran into the kitchen to light a lamp. There King Chili and his men were waiting for him. They threw chili powder in his eyes and blinded him. The monster covered his eyes, howling with pain. Then King Tortoise and his men blew out the lamp.

The monster was so frightened that he ran out of the kitchen door, but King Pumpkin and his men were waiting on the overhanging roof. They all rolled off and dropped right on the monster's head. Then King Bee and his subjects dove down and stung the monster's face.

The monster let out a great scream and ran right back through the house and out the front door. But when he went down the front steps, he slipped on King Moss and his subjects and rolled right to the bottom.

At the foot of the steps, Ba Kho was waiting with his

gleaming knife. With one mighty stroke, Ba Kho cut off the monster's head.

The monster was dead! The victorious army went in procession to the village to announce the good news.

At the head of the procession, flew King Bee and his subjects. On the ground, King Chili and his red men came first, followed by King Pumpkin and the pumpkin army. King Snake followed with King Tortoise. Last of all came Ba Kho, who was so tired from killing the monster that he could hardly walk.

But Ba Kho was very happy. In the village, men, women, and children stood waiting along the streets to welcome them. King Monkey had spied on them, and had gone ahead to tell the people the good news.

The villagers welcomed Ba Kho and his friends as heroes, and they all celebrated the death of the monster for three days and three nights.

What Are Friends for?

(a story from India)

A poor farmer had been away from home for many months. There was no work in his village, so he had been forced to leave his family to find work in town. He had worked hard and saved, and now he was returning home with his savings tucked into his dhoti.

The sun was a blazing ball of fire overhead and the farmer was exhausted. "A few minutes' rest will give me strength to finish my journey," he said to himself, and he sank down against the trunk of a shady fig tree. He stretched out his weary legs, closed his eyes, and was soon fast asleep.

"Grr . . . grr . . . grrr!" A strange, low growling woke him.

"What's that? What's that?" he mumbled, half asleep, turning his head from side to side.

"Gr . . . grr . . . grr-oaw!" The strange rasping cough grew louder.

The farmer could hear the crackling of branches as something moved heavily above him. He opened his eyes wide and looked up. There was a large brown bear climbing down the tree towards him!

"Ahhhhh!" the farmer groaned, shutting his eyes tight and holding his breath. Frozen stiff with fright, he searched wildly in his mind for a way to escape. "If I get up and run, the bear will chase me and catch me. If I stay where I am, the bear will leap on top of me. Let me be brave. I will stand and fight the bear!" And he pulled himself up slowly, his back still against the tree.

The poor, trembling farmer looked up again. The bear was very close to him. It hugged the trunk with both arms as it came down the tree. When it reached the bottom, the farmer moved to the opposite side of the tree and grabbed hold of the bear's paws. The tree trunk was between them as they faced each other. The farmer held one of the bear's paws tight in each hand and they circled slowly around and around the tree as if they were dancing. As they moved, the coins that had been carefully tucked away in the farmer's dhoti fell tinkling to the ground, one at a time.

At that moment, a rich moneylender was passing by. As soon as he heard the tinkling of the coins, he stopped. He traced the sweet sound of money to the shady fig tree and when he looked closely, he couldn't believe his eyes. The farmer and the bear, solemnly facing each other, were moving around and around the tree in graceful harmony, one step at a time. And they were holding hands! The moneylender's jaw fell open in astonishment.

"A man and a bear dancing around a tree together!" he exclaimed. "And on the ground a heap of glittering coins which no one has bothered to pick up?"

The moneylender gazed lovingly at the coins. Then he approached the farmer. "Dear friend," he said, his voice as smooth and as sweet as honey. "I've never seen such a strange sight. Please tell me what's happening."

The poor farmer was circling the tree thinking sadly, *Will I ever see my family again?*

When he heard the moneylender's silky voice, he replied quickly. "Ah, my good friend. You say it's a strange sight? Wait till I tell you the whole story. You won't believe it!"

The moneylender moved closer, licking his lips.

"The coins you see on the ground come from the bear," said the farmer.

"From the bear?" echoed the moneylender.

"Yes!" said the farmer. "From the bear. Each time we go around the tree, money drops from the bear's backside. The more times we go around, the more money comes out.

The moneylender's eyes lit up with greed as he thought, *Here's an easy way to make money. It won't be difficult to trick this simple fellow.* Then, tapping the farmer gently on the shoulder, his voice full of tenderness, he whispered, "You look tired, my good friend, going around and around and around. Let me help you. I'll take your place while you have a rest. After all, what are friends for?"

Wearily, the poor farmer nodded and the moneylender eagerly took his place, grabbing the bear's paws firmly in his own hands. Immediately, they started to move around the tree trunk in circles—the rich moneylender and the bear.

Heaving a great sigh of relief, the poor farmer gathered up all of his coins from the ground. He tied them firmly into his dhoti once again and set off for home. Just before he turned on to the main path, he looked back. The rich moneylender was still smiling sweetly, holding the bear's paws firmly in his hands, the tree between them, going around and around and around . . .